Ten Poems
about Bal

ex libris

Candlestick Press

Published by:
Candlestick Press,
Diversity House, 72 Nottingham Road, Arnold, Nottingham NG5 6LF
www.candlestickpress.co.uk

Design, typesetting, print and production by Diversity Creative
Marketing Solutions Ltd., www.diversitymarketing.co.uk

Introduction and selection © Imtiaz Dharker, 2015

Cover illustration, 'Baby in a Car Seat', wood engraving,
1996 © Beth Krommes, www.bethkrommes.com

© Candlestick Press, 2015

ISBN 978 1 907598 30 2

Candlestick Press wishes to thank Imtiaz Dharker for her generosity.

Acknowledgements:
Sylvia Plath, 'You're' is reprinted from *Ariel*, copyright © 1961 by Ted
Hughes by permission of HarperCollins Publishers in the USA and
elsewhere by permission of Faber & Faber Ltd. Don Paterson, 'Waking
with Russell' is reprinted from *Landing Light*, copyright © 2005 by Don
Paterson, reprinted with the permission of The Permissions Company,
Inc., on behalf of Graywolf Press, www.graywolfpress.org in the USA.
Elsewhere, it is reprinted from Don Paterson, *Landing Light* (Faber & Faber,
2003) © 2003 Don Paterson by kind permission of Faber & Faber Ltd.
John Agard, 'Moonbelly' from *Alternative Anthem: Selected Poems with
Live DVD* (Bloodaxe Books, 2009) is reprinted with permission of Bloodaxe
Books, on behalf of the author; Maura Dooley, 'Freight' from *Sound
Barrier: Poems 1982 – 2002* (Bloodaxe Books, 2002)) is reprinted with
permission of Bloodaxe Books, on behalf of the author; Anne Stevenson,
'The Victory' from *Poems 1955 – 2005* (Bloodaxe Books, 2005) is reprinted
with permission of Bloodaxe Books, on behalf of the author, and
Imtiaz Dharker, 'First Words' from *Over the Moon* (Bloodaxe Books, 2014)
is reprinted with permission of Bloodaxe Books, on behalf of the author.
Kate Clanchy, 'Not Art' from *Newborn* (Picador, 2004) is reprinted by
kind permission of Pan Macmillan and is copyright © Kate Clanchy, 2004.
Gillian Clarke, 'Baby-sitting' from *Collected Poems* (Carcanet Press, 1997)
is reprinted by kind permission of Carcanet Press and Carol Ann Duffy,
'A Child's Sleep' from *New Selected Poems* (Picador, 2004) is reprinted by
kind permission of the author.

While every effort has been made to secure permission to reprint material
protected by copyright, we will be pleased to make good any omissions
brought to our attention in future printings of this pamphlet.

Where poets are no longer living, their dates are given.

Introduction

When it came to choosing my most loved *Ten Poems about Babies*, my first wish-list was thirty poems long and could have been at least three times longer; but these were the ones I kept coming back to, perhaps because something in them triggered a memory of that exact baby smell, the weight of the head on the chest, the exhaustion and confusion of feelings, the havoc and wonder that surrounds such a coming.

I also had the luxury of choosing poems where the language doesn't just describe the experience but extends and enriches it. Sylvia Plath's 'You're' has a first verse that tumbles along as if the poem is trying to become the baby, to make itself in the womb and arrive warm and edible as 'my little loaf'. The poets here go far beyond easy sentimentality: the baby is described as anything from 'our travelled prawn', a 'drumseed a-bloom', 'little dancing bones' or 'close work', to 'tiny antagonist' and even the grudging 'perfectly acceptable child'. These babies are not idealised, but lived with and given close attention, the poet's scrutiny rewarded as Don Paterson's is in 'Waking with Russell', '…the true gift never leaves the giver:/ returned and redelivered, it rolled on/ until the smile poured through us like a river.'

These poems have been able to take on the mystery as well as the reality of a new being coming into the world, and it is an exhilarating sweep from the moment of conception in John Agard's 'Moonbelly' to Kate Clanchy's 'prising of muck from the grain of the floor'; from Gillian Clarke's truthfully 'wrong baby' to Carol Ann Duffy's supremely right one, and the sacred peace of 'A Child's Sleep', 'both open palms/ cupping their soft light'.

Imtiaz Dharker

You're

Clownlike, happiest on your hands,
Feet to the stars, and moon-skulled,
Gilled like a fish. A common-sense
Thumbs-down on the dodo's mode.
Wrapped up in yourself like a spool,
Trawling your dark as owls do.
Mute as a turnip from the Fourth
Of July to All Fools' Day,
O high-riser, my little loaf.

Vague as fog and looked for like mail.
Farther off than Australia.
Bent-backed Atlas, our travelled prawn.
Snug as a bud and at home
Like a sprat in a pickle jug.
A creel of eels, all ripples.
Jumpy as a Mexican bean.
Right, like a well-done sum.
A clean slate, with your own face on.

Sylvia Plath (1932 – 1963)

Moonbelly

Drumseed
a-bloom
wit de speed
of water
daddywater
meet
mummywater
in one twinkling
monthly blood
turn back
it own tide

monthly blood
have new mouth
to feed

a new mouth is new bud

when mummywater
an daddywater
meet

Wit good blessing
spirits willing
navel string
soon sing

John Agard

Freight

I am the ship in which you sail,
little dancing bones,
your passage between the dream
and the waking dream,
your sieve, your pea-green boat.
I'll pay whatever toll your ferry needs.
And you, whose history's already charted
in a rope of cells, be tender to
those other unnamed vessels
who will surprise you one day,
tug-tugging, irresistible,
and float you out beyond your depth,
where you'll look down, puzzled, amazed.

Maura Dooley

Infant Joy

I have no name
I am but two days old.
What shall I call thee?
I happy am
Joy is my name,
Sweet joy befall thee!

Pretty joy!
Sweet joy but two days old,
Sweet joy I call thee;
Thou dost smile.
I sing the while
Sweet joy befall thee.

William Blake (1757 - 1827)

Not Art

This is close work, this babystuff,
the intricate wiping and wrapping, the slow
unpicking of miniature fists;
village-work, a hand-craft, all bodges
and spit, the gains inchingly small
as the knotting of carpets, raw wool
rasping in the teeth of the comb.

The strewing and stooping, the prising
of muck from the grain of the floor -
I think of gleaners, ash-sifters, of tents
sewn with shoe soles, wedding veils, plaits,
how patchwork is stitched-up detritus,
how it circles on quilts like the bits
of a house in a typhoon's trail.

And the ache in the neck, in the back,
in the foot, are the knocks of wood looms,
narrow as cradles, borne from pasture
to valley to camp. I am learning
the art of mistakes, to accept
every evening that the marks of the day
are woven in too far back to pick out.

This is the work women draw from the river,
wet to the waist, singing in time,
the work we swing from our shoulders,
lay on the ground and let the crowd
hold and finger and weigh up - the young girls
wondering, the laughing old women,
the halt, the milk-eyed, the blind.

Kate Clanchy

The Victory

I thought you were my victory
though you cut me like a knife
when I brought you out of my body
into your life.

Tiny antagonist, gory,
blue as a bruise. The stains
of your cloud of glory
bled from my veins.

How can you dare, blind thing,
blank insect eyes?
You barb the air. You sting
with bladed cries.

Snail. Scary knot of desires.
Hungry snarl. Small son.
Why do I have to love you?
How have you won?

Anne Stevenson

Waking with Russell

Whatever the difference is, it all began
the day we woke up face-to-face like lovers
and his four-day-old smile dawned on him again,
possessed him, till it would not fall or waver;
and I pitched back not my old hard-pressed grin
but his own smile, or one I'd rediscovered.
Dear son, I was *mezzo del cammin*
and the true path was as lost to me as ever
when you cut in front and lit it as you ran.
See how the true gift never leaves the giver:
returned and redelivered, it rolled on
until the smile poured through us like a river.
How fine, I thought, this waking amongst men!
I kissed your mouth and pledged myself forever.

Don Paterson

Baby-sitting

I am sitting in a strange room listening
For the wrong baby. I don't love
This baby. She is sleeping a snuffly
Roseate, bubbling sleep; she is fair;
She is a perfectly acceptable child.
I am afraid of her. If she wakes
She will hate me. She will shout
Her hot midnight rage, her nose
Will stream disgustingly and the perfume
Of her breath will fail to enchant me.

To her I will represent absolute
Abandonment. For her it will be worse
Than for the lover cold in lonely
Sheets; worse than for the woman who waits
A moment to collect her dignity
Beside the bleached bone in the terminal ward.
As she rises sobbing from the monstrous land
Stretching for milk-familiar comforting,
She will find me and between us two
It will not come. It will not come.

Gillian Clarke

First words

for Ava

Her fingers scrabble at glass,
over floorboards, table legs and chairs
to catch the word that runs away from her,
sifted through leaves, snatched up on a breeze,
stolen by clouds, returned.

Propelled on bottom, elbows, knees,
with silent determination, she follows it
and only when it spills out of her hand,
whispers, like someone in a church
or library, *sunshine*.

She knows the moon even when
it is nothing more than a curl on blue,
or half an ear listening for the next star.
Even the disc of milk in a bowl is *moon*.
She says the word and drinks it in.

Imtiaz Dharker

A Child's Sleep

I stood at the edge of my child's sleep
hearing her breathe;
although I could not enter there,
I could not leave.

Her sleep was a small wood,
perfumed with flowers;
dark, peaceful, sacred,
acred in hours.

And she was the spirit that lives
in the heart of such woods;
without time, without history,
wordlessly good.

I spoke her name, a pebble dropped
in the still night,
and saw her stir, both open palms
cupping their soft light;

then went to the window. The greater dark
outside the room
gazed back, maternal, wise,
with its face of moon.

Carol Ann Duffy